How to play the game

The year is 50 BC. Gaul is entirely occupied by the Romans. Well, not entirely ... One small village of indomitable Gauls still holds out against the invaders. And life is not easy for the Roman legionaries who garrison the fortified camps of Totorum, Aquarium, Laudanum and Compendium ...

Over to you!

Dogmatix is hidden in each of the scenes in this book. Are your powers of observation really good? It's up to you to find the clever little dog who is Obelix's faithful companion – in the village, in the forest, on land, at sea or in the air. And there are plenty of other surprises as well!

The challenge:

Look carefully at the pictures in this book — they are a real challenge!

Whenever you find Dogmatix, you win 2 golden bones.

For tracking down five of the six other characters shown to the left of each scene, you score 1 golden bone each.

Identifying the character who doesn't appear in the picture scores 3 golden bones. When you've finished, count up your bones.

If you have won between 80 and 120 golden bones, you're the champion!

And good luck, by Toutatis!

Asterix   Obelix   Dogmatix   Impedimenta   Vitalstatistix   Unhygienix   Cacofonix   Fulliautomatix

Mrs Fulliautomatix   Mrs Geriatrix   Geriatrix   Anticlimax   Polysyllabix   Fotogenix   Panacea

Bacteria

Boneywasawarriorwayayix

Winesanspirix

Justforkix

Histrionix

Bucolix

Pepe

Pegleg

Håråldwilssen

Nøgøødreåssen

Ødiuscømpårissen

Steptøånssen

Herendethelessen

Sourpus

Claphamomnibus

Caesar

Odoriferus

Garrulus Vinus

Crismus Cactus

Nautilus

Bogus Genius

Courtingdisastus

Salamix

Spurius Brontosaurus

Infectius Virus

Dubius Status

Cumulonimbus

WHO SAYS MY FISH PONGS?

There's nothing like a good fish fight to start the day and keep you fit. When Unhygienix gets out his stock of fish, all of them genuine antiques, Fulliautomatix and the others are soon in the middle of a game of pong-pong. They'll have a slap-up fish breakfast!

All these characters except one are in the picture. Who is the odd one out?

x10

THE WILD BOAR HUNT

After limbering up with the fish fight, the Gauls set out on a boar hunt. Chasing boar is never a bore – there's nothing our friends like better, unless it's chasing Romans.

All these characters except one are in the picture. Who is the odd one out?

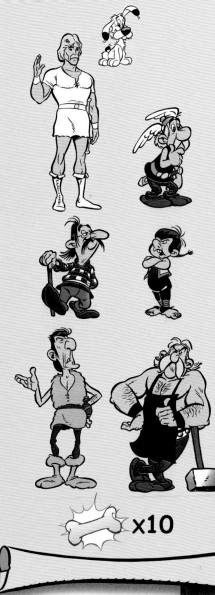

x10

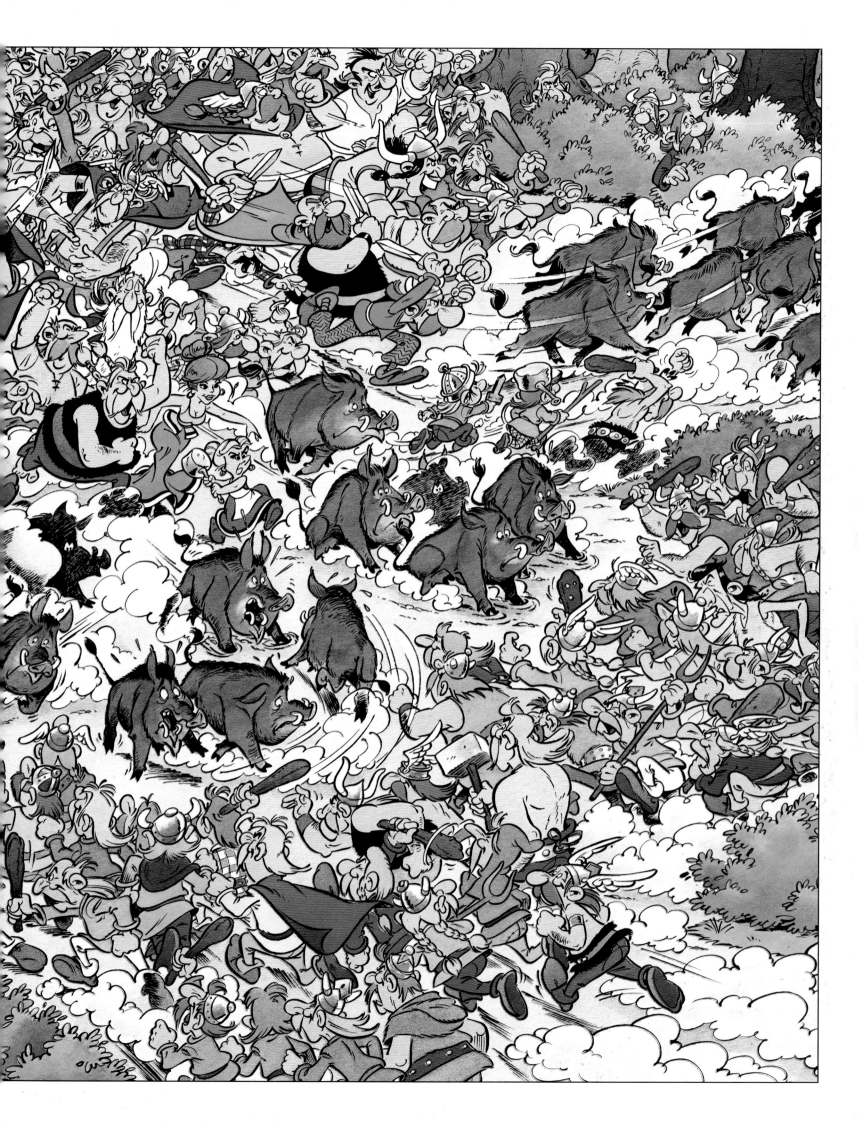

A DOSE OF MAGIC POTION

Out in the forest, Asterix and Obelix have spotted some Romans. Getafix brews his potion and gives all the villagers a dose . . . except for Obelix, who, as usual, has to go without. It works like magic for the others.

All these characters except one are in the picture. Who is the odd one out?

x10

COMBAT STATIONS!

In their famous tortoise formation, the Romans are ready for anything. But so are the Gauls, now that they're full of magic potion. In the thick of the fray, tempers fray.

All these characters except one are in the picture. Who is the odd one out?

THE ROMANS ATTACK

Biff! Boing! The Gauls are having a wonderful time in the thick of battle! And it's no picnic for the Romans. Even their packed wild-boar lunch is running away.

All these characters except one are in the picture. Who is the odd one out?

x10

THE GAULS STRIKE BACK

The indomitable Gauls have hardly even warmed up, but by now things are getting too hot for the Romans. Maybe a visit to the fortified Roman camp of Totorum will give the Gauls some more fun.

All these characters except one are in the picture. Who is the odd one out?

x10

IT'S A KNOCK-OUT!

The Gauls came, they fought,
they conquered. It's official:
the Roman legions are flattened.
They've been counted out!
Our friends are happy to know
that Caesar will be furious.

All these characters except
one are in the picture.
Who is the odd one out?

x10

IN CONDATUM

A little stroll around the town of Condatum before going to sea, one more punch-up for the road, and a few legionaries sent flying, keep our Gaulish friends fit and in rude health – too rude for these Romans.

All these characters except one are in the picture. Who is the odd one out?

x10

A BOARDING PARTY!

On their boating excursion, the Gauls spot a Norman longship on its way to invade. Some of the Normans float, some paddle, some sink – and the Gauls' trip to the seaside is going swimmingly.

All these characters except one are in the picture. Who is the odd one out?

x10

WELCOME HOME!

Asterix and Obelix come home to the village in triumph. It's Happy Hour – knocking back a few Romans will give everyone a good appetite for the banquet.

All these characters except one are in the picture. Who is the odd one out?

x10

THESE ROMANS ARE SPHERICAL!

The Romans think they will bounce back, but once again they have a hard time. They have been drinking an unusual potion which leaves them as round as balls. Can they have been bowled over by one of Getafix's magic ingredients?

All these characters except one are in the picture. Who is the odd one out?

x10

A BANQUET DANCE

After leading the Romans a merry dance all day, the Gauls dance at their own banquet, under the starry sky where the god Toutatis lives.
On the menu: barley beer and roast boar, leaving them stoked up for another good day's Roman-thumping tomorrow.

All these characters except one are in the picture. Who is the odd one out?

x10

A BANQUET DANCE

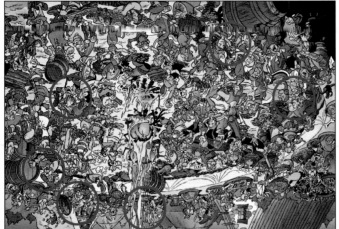

THESE ROMANS ARE SPHERICAL!

WELCOME HOME!

A BOARDING PARTY

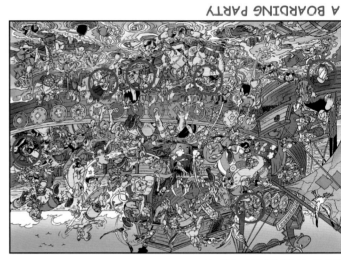

IN CONDATUM

IT'S A KNOCK-OUT!

THE GAULS STRIKE BACK

THE ROMANS ATTACK

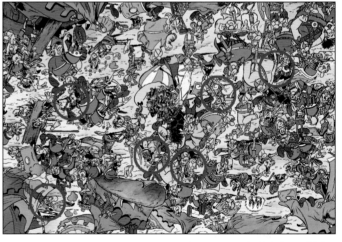

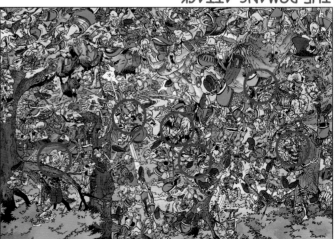

COMBAT STATIONS!

A DOSE OF MAGIC POTION

THE WILD BOAR HUNT

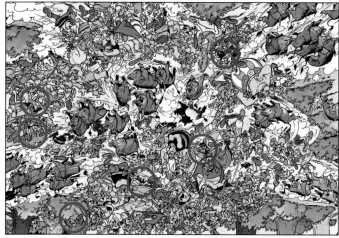

WHO SAYS MY FISH PONGS?

Also available in this series:

Where's Asterix?

Original title: *Cherche et Trouve Idéfix*
Original edition © 2010 Les Éditions Albert René/
Goscinny-Uderzo
Text and layouts © 2010 Hachette Livre
English translation © 2012 Hachette Livre

Exclusive licensee: Orion Publishing Group
Translator: Anthea Bell

English translation first published in 2012
This paperback edition first published in 2013
by Orion Children's Books
a division of the Orion Publishing Group Ltd
Orion House
5 Upper St Martin's Lane
London WC2H 9EA

An Hachette UK company

1 3 5 7 9 10 8 6 4 2

Printed in China
The Orion Publishing Group's policy is to use papers
that are natural, renewable and recyclable products made
from wood grown in sustainable forests. The logging and
manufacturing processes are expected to conform to the
environmental regulations of the country of origin.

www.asterix.com
www.orionbooks.co.uk

A CIP Catalogue record for this book is available
from the British Library
ISBN 978 1 4440 0843 2